RAISE THE DRAWBRIDGE

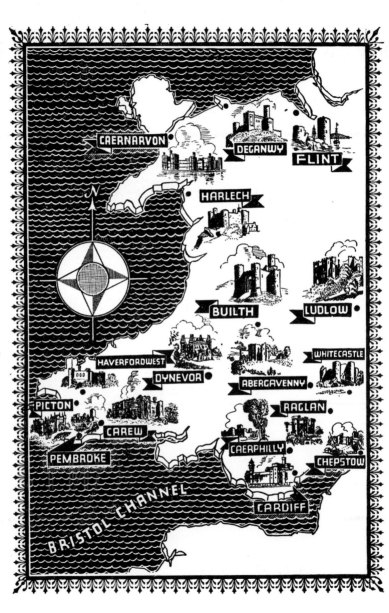

RAISE THE DRAWBRIDGE

STORIES AND LEGENDS
OF WELSH CASTLES

BY

BERYL M. JONES

*With illustrations by
Geoffrey Evans*

JOHN JONES PUBLISHING LTD

RAISE THE DRAWBRIDGE

by Beryl M. Jones

This new paperback edition published March 1999
Text and cover design copyright John Jones Publishing Ltd
First published in 1938 by *The Western Mail*

ISBN 1 871083 76 1

Cover design by Olwen Fowler

Published by John Jones Publishing Ltd.,
Unit 12, Clwydfro Business Centre, Ruthin,
North Wales LL15 1NJ

Printed in Wales by Dinefwr Press,
Llandybie, Carmarthenshire SA18 3YD

AUTHOR'S NOTE

Castles have played an important part in the history of Wales. To-day most of them stand in silent ruin and only through tale and legend can we imagine the stirring incidents that took place within their walls.

This book has been written for children in order to portray in story form the most interesting events connected with some of our castles.

I wish here to express my deep gratitude to Professor William Rees, M.A., D.Sc., Professor of the History of Wales, University College, Cardiff, and to Mr. A. G. Prys-Jones, M.A., for the advice they gave me and for their help in revising the proofs.

B.M.J.

p. 16 The rescued Welsh king GRUFFYD AP CYNAN was your great-x-29-grandfather

p. 23 In 1138 King Henry I's successor King Stephen bestowed the castle and earldom of Pembroke on your great-x-30-grandfather GILBERT DE CLARE, "Strongbow", along with the castle and earldom of Striguil (aka Chepstow, p. 129). Both castles remained in the possession of our ancestors for many generations.

p.31 It was not really Walter but your great-x-28 grandfather G28 GILBERT DE LACY who in the Romance of Fulk Fitzwarine attacked Ludlow Castle. During the war King Stephen had taken Ludlow Castle away from him and bestowed it on Josse de Dinant. But Henry II gave it back to him, and it remained the home of our De Lacy & Mortimer ancestors for many generations. You are also descended from Walter de Lacy, whether Gilbert's grandfather or his grandson.

p. 55 WILLIAM DE BRAOSE was your great-x-27 grandfather.

p. 84. HUGH LE DESPENSER was your great-x-25-grandfather. King Edward II and his queen Isabella were your G23s.

p.99 Harlech Castle actually surrendered in 1468 to a siege by your G18 WILLIAM, LORD HERBERT, a leading Yorkist supporter of Edward IV, who a month later created him Earl of Pembroke. But it was his more compassionate younger brother Sir Richard Herbert who after the surrender arranged to spare the governor's life.

p. 113 Raglan castle was our ancestral home from 1440 until 1646, when your Cavalier great-x-12-grandfather HENRY SOMERSET, 5th Earl & 1st Marquis of Worcester, aged 85, defended it for 2 months against the Roundhead siege. Then destroyed, it has since been a picturesque but uninhabited ruin.

CONTENTS

GEOFFREY EVANS

WHITECASTLE

During the 11th century William Rufus, the Red King, continued the conquest of Wales after the death of his father, William the Conquerer. His Norman barons, superior in arms and training, treated the Welsh rulers with contempt.

1

THE BLIND KNIGHT
OF WHITECASTLE

In early days, when William Rufus was King of England, the Welsh were seething with anger because of the invasion of their fair valleys and domains by the powerful Norman lords.

Whitecastle was then the home of an aged Welsh knight named Gwyn ap Gwaethfoed. The knight was blind, but that did not prevent his joining in the hunt or visiting his brothers who lived in the castles of Skenfrith and Grosmont in Monmouthshire. These three castles had been built in a triangle to form a stronghold against the hated Normans.

One day, when the blind knight was away from his castle, a bold Norman baron, taking advantage of the fact that the lord was absent, laid siege to the castle, and, in a short while, took possession.

That evening, as the red sun set over the tree-clad hill, Gwyn rode gaily homewards. But before he reached Whitecastle, he was met by Rolant, one of his archers.

"Alack, my lord," cried Rolant, "to-day your fair castle has been captured by a troop of thieving Norman soldiers. On your life, you dare not ride thither."

Gwyn passed his hands across his sightless eyes. "How now, Rolant, are you afraid of a handful of cowardly foreigners? Go, summon our men, bid them gather up their pikes, bows and lances, and any weapon they can lay their hands upon. We'll show these Norman knaves of what stuff Welshmen are made."

Rolant the Archer caught at his master's bridle. "Nay," he cried, "we are far outnumbered. It is folly to match our men against them. Besides, the portcullis is down and the drawbridge already drawn, and who knows better than ourselves how useless it is to batter against the strong fortress of Whitecastle?"

"Then take my horse," commanded Gwyn, "and ride to every castle until you find Rufus the King. Tell him an aged knight claims the right to fight fairly for his castle. I beg leave to engage in single combat with this upstart Norman baron."

"But, my lord—you forget—," faltered Rolant, "you are blind; what chance would you have against one whose eyes are as keen as a hawk's?"

"Then we will both be thus handicapped," replied Gwyn. "Tell the King I would fight this Norman in a darkened room in the tower of Whitecastle."

" But your age," continued Rolant, " he is young I know, and as sturdy as the oak."

" Aye, but not stouter-hearted than I," came the quick reply. " Haste, if you would serve me, and may the braver win."

Rolant the Archer leapt swiftly upon his master's horse and sped on his mission. Meanwhile, the days passed and the blind knight grew more and more embittered as he heard the strange tongue of the Norman soldiers who walked to and from his beloved castle.

At last, the faithful Rolant returned with permission from the King for the strange duel to take place. The message was swiftly sent to the Norman Baron, who haughtily replied, " I hear this Welshman is both old and blind. Tell him I do not wish to have his blood upon my hands. Since he has no chance of victory, I advise him to forget the challenge and to ride with all haste from Whitecastle."

The plain costume similar to that worn by the Norman lady of this period.

G. E.

But Gwyn was already riding over the drawbridge into the courtyard.

Unaided, he dismounted and called upon the Norman baron to lead the way up to the darkened chamber in the tower. With bad grace, the younger man did so, and, climbing the winding steps, the two entered a small room whose lancets had previously been filled with mud and stone. And the faithful Rolant, keeping close to his master's heels, saw to it that not a single ray of light pierced the gloom.

As the two duellists bared their swords, Rolant closed the door and waited with the group of Norman soldiers who had climbed the tower in order to catch any sounds of the fight.

" I'll wager my coat of mail that my lord wins," cried one of the Norman soldiers. Not understanding the foreign tongue, but guessing the meaning from the jeering looks of the others, Rolant made signs that he would wager his right arm.

No shout or cry escaped from the darkened room, only the clash of steel and the quick footsteps of the two as they leapt here and darted there, each parrying to deliver the fatal thrust.

At last, the soldiers heard the sound of someone falling heavily to the floor. The soldiers leapt to their feet and motionlessly stared at the closed door. Rolant stood alone, a

Out stepped the blind knight and, with a cry of delight, Rolant leapt towards him.

rigid figure, his lips set in a firm line. Norman and Welshman breathlessly awaited the rightful owner of Whitecastle.

There was a pause and slowly the door was opened. Out stepped the blind knight and, with a cry of delight, Rolant leaped towards him. For a moment, the victor stood with head raised high, then as the amazed cries of Norman soldiers reached his ears, he shouted, " Out upon you, harsh voiced thieves!"

Then, as though his blind eyes could see the scared looks on the faces of the Normans as they raced head-long down the winding steps and out through the gates, Gwyn ap Gwaethfoed laughed aloud.

And, leaning on the staunch shoulders of faithful Rolant the Archer, the blind Lord of Whitecastle proudly descended his tower.

FROM AN OLD PRINT
G F.

DEGANWY

The Normans feared Gruffydd, a ruler of
North Wales, who had successfully resisted
them.   By a trick they lured him from
Gwynedd and carried him off to Chester.
This incident took place during the 11th
century.

15

2

A WELSH
KING IS AVENGED

It was fair day in ancient Chester.

The ways of the city were thronged with buyers and sellers and with idlers. The market-place was full of noisy, jostling customers, and every person, whether peasant or lord, was attired in holiday dress.

Even the keepers of the walls and castle had neglected their posts to while away the hours in watching the games and other pleasantries.

Down the busy thoroughfare a tall, young Welsh chieftain pushed his way towards the castle. He was head and shoulders taller than most men, and his name was Cynric Hir, or Cynric the Tall. A rough cloak swung from his broad shoulders and many an admiring glance was cast after the young giant.

At last, he reached the castle gates and saw a lame beggar standing near the deserted gateway.

" I seek Gruffydd ap Cynan," said the young man, in a low voice. " He has been a prisoner here in

The men of this period adopted semi-circular cloaks and wore shoes with narrow toes which curled up at the ends.

Chester Castle for many years. Think you I can speak with him?"

"I often hear the guardsmen chaff about this Gruffydd," replied the beggar. "He claims to be a Welsh King!"

"And so he is!" retorted Cynric fiercely, "It was Hugh the Wolf, your brutal Earl of Chester, who captured him and brought him here. And while he suffers in some evil dungeon, Hugh's nephew, Robert of Rhuddlan, plunders his fair land."

"He has suffered enough," said the beggar. "At first I used to hear him trying to tear the cruel chains from his body, but of late he has grown so weak that he does not even murmur."

"Have you seen him, then?" cried Cynric eagerly.

The beggar looked around, but the sentries were still out of sight and, pointing to a narrow slit in the wall some distance further on, he shuffled on his way.

Cynric raced to the spot and peered through the narrow opening in the steep wall. At last, through the

He lifted him with ease upon his massive shoulders.

gloom, he could dimly see a huddled form lying on the ground.

" Courage ! " whispered Cynric. " I am your kinsman come to free you."

Feebly the figure stirred ; then a weak voice answered, " I cannot live much longer. Go, before they return. If they find you here, Hugh the Wolf will torture you to death."

Without further word, Cynric stole beneath the wall and slipped into the deserted castle. It took some time to reach the dungeon where the Welsh King lay, but, at last he came upon the great door. Luckily, the door was easily forced open, for the guards had long ceased to keep a strict watch on one who had grown so weak and ill from the weight of his bonds.

" You will never break my bonds," whispered Gruffydd. " See how they have worn into my flesh."

Cynric's heart ached at the terrible sight, but he said firmly, " Speak not a word until we are out of Chester."

Picking up the king's worn body in his strong young arms, he lifted him with ease upon his massive shoulders.

Then, flinging his wide cloak over all, he carried his precious burden out of the dungeon.

Fortunately, the sentries and guards were still enjoying their games and Cynric walked boldly out of the castle of Hugh the Wolf. He did not dare rest until he had left noisy Chester far behind and was safely across the River Dee.

Once in Wales, willing friends sheltered Gruffydd and released him from the cruel bonds. Daily Cynric tended him, but it was many months before the enfeebled king was strong again. The two then made their home in a mountain cave, for Robert of Rhuddlan, Hugh the Wolf's nephew, had taken possession of the Welsh king's land. There they plotted with their followers to avenge themselves for the King's imprisonment.

To attempt warfare on the mighty Earl of Chester was futile, but an attack on Robert would be an easier matter, especially when they heard that he was now living in his castle at Deganwy.

The two soon procured ships and men and they decided to surprise Robert by sailing into the mouth of the Conway River and landing near his castle. It was a warm, summer day when Gruffydd and young Cynric landed with their supporters, and Robert was fast asleep in his castle.

" Behold the stolen cattle ! " cried Cynric, pointing to where a vast herd of sleek black cattle grazed on the slopes above the river.

" And the stolen sheep ! " said another, pointing to a fine flock of woolly sheep penned near the castle walls.

" Come," said Gruffydd, " let us load them on to our ships, for I vow most of them are ours."

Robert must have been sleeping soundly indeed, for he did not hear the cries of the animals as they were driven down the beach. At last, however, one of his servants aroused him.

" Awake ! " he cried. " A raid ! a raid ! A horde of invaders are making off with your best sheep and cattle ! "

Robert sprang to the window and saw the Welshmen's ships laden with his animals. In great rage, he snatched his spear and shield and ran from the castle calling upon his men to keep up with him. " Marauders ! Plunderers ! " Robert shouted after them as the first ship began to sail away.

" Many are the vales he has pillaged," cried young Cynric, " yet see in what fury he grows because we have taken our own back."

As Robert came racing madly down to the beach, a shower of javelins poured upon him from one of the ships, and immediately he fell wounded to the ground.

Proudly the last ship rode the tide, bearing with it the avenged Welsh king and brave Cynric the Tall. And together they watched that still figure upon the beach, until the shore and the frowning castle above were slowly lost to sight.

PEMBROKE

GEOFFREY EVANS

After their victories, the Normans built castles on the border which they found was the strongest means of keeping the Welsh in check. Henry I was King of England when Gerald of Windsor was left in charge of Pembroke Castle.

3

THE "WIZARD" OF PEMBROKE

In the 11th century, a Norman Earl, Arnulf of Montgomery, marched into Pembrokeshire.

Espying a rocky headland, he acclaimed it a fine spot for a fortress, to keep the Welsh chieftains in check. And so on the site where the massive walls of Pembroke Castle now stand was built a fortress of stout stakes and goodly turf.

After a while, Earl Arnulf tired of his castle by the sea, and, calling to his faithful castellan, Gerald of Windsor, cried, " I long to set foot in fair England again. Will you guard my castle while I am away ? "

" With my life ! " replied the worthy Gerald readily, but, knowing too well the power of the Welsh to deliver sudden attacks, added, " These native Welsh princes are ever watchful, my lord. Once they learn you are away, they will rise together to capture the castle." At this Arnulf smiled, " I leave my castle in worthy hands, Gerald. Bear in mind, while I am away, that Normans defend their castles by cunning."

As Gerald expected, no sooner had his master set foot on English soil than the suppressed native princes of South Wales arose and laid siege to the castle. Gerald strengthened the walls and barricaded the entrances of the fortress. All went well with him until, one night, fifteen of his soldiers cruelly deserted him and stole from the castle in a boat.

In the meantime, increasing numbers of Welsh troops gathered outside the castle of Pembroke, but so bravely did Gerald and his small force hold out against them, that several weeks passed by without a sign of surrender.

" If we cannot force them out we'll starve them out ! " cried one of the Welsh princes. "Their food supply cannot last much longer."

With her hair in long plaits and extra long sleeves to her dress, women of this period were attractively dressed.

He spoke truly, for already the garrison within the castle was half starved. Only four

hogs remained, and these Gerald ordered to be roasted at once.

" Ho, ho, we're in for a right hearty meal at last ! " One of the soldiers smacked his lips. " I could eat a whole hog with ease myself."

But Gerald, hearing of the enemy's boast, had other plans for disposing of the hogs. When they were roasted, he bade his men carry them to the top of the barricade that overlooked the enemy's camp. Outside, the Welsh soldiers sat in little groups, their weapons idle, since they considered that starving a garrison into surrender was not only the surest way to capture a castle, but also the easiest.

As one of them saw Gerald upon the castle wall, he shouted, " Aye, already they beg for food. What say you to a goodly deer in exchange for the castle?"

In answer, Gerald, although he himself longed to feast off one of the hogs, bade his soldiers take their sharpest knives and, cutting off pieces of the meat, fling them to the Welsh soldiers.

" But 'tis a sinful waste ! " cried one of his men. " We are starving ! Why throw good meat to our enemies ? "

The letter showed up clearly in the moonlight and, as the sentry drew near, he pounced upon it.

" A Norman defends his castle by cunning," replied Gerald, and, as he too, cut off the meat and flung it to the amazed Welshmen, his soldiers reluctantly followed suit.

At sight of this, one of the Welsh princes exclaimed, " We were mistaken ! These Normans have so much food they can afford to fling it away ! "

" We'll never starve them into surrender ! " cried another. " Come, let us go home."

But the others determined to stand their ground for a while longer, and refused to move away from the castle.

Desperate now, for not a single loaf remained, Gerald thought of another ruse to rid the castle of its enemy. That night, he wrote a letter and addressed it to the Bishop of St. David's, who, at that time, was staying in the neighbourhood.

That night, he cautiously slipped from the castle and stole towards the Welsh camp. He crept warily, for the moon was up and cast its white light upon the pathway. He stole to the spot where he had often watched the Welsh sentry march to and fro. Flinging the parchment scroll into the sentry's path, he hid close by.

The letter showed up clearly in the moonlight, and as the sentry drew near, he pounced upon it. Seeing it was sealed with Gerald of Windsor's signet, he raced with it to his chieftain, who, eagerly bursting it open for news from the castle, read aloud the passage that ran :—

" And so since my garrison can easily hold out for

at least another four months, I see no need that you should summon my lord Arnulf to our aid."

" Another four months ! " gasped the Welsh prince. " Why, this Gerald of Windsor must be a wizard conjuring his food supplies out of thin air ! "

" Pah ! " cried another ; " I'll not linger here for another four months. Come, let us depart."

Swiftly the news spread around the astonished Welsh camp, and one and all agreed to disperse from the castle whose garrison could so mysteriously hold out against them.

So at dawn Gerald, peering from the fortress, joy-fully beheld the Welsh gathering up their possessions. Occasionally, the Welsh soldiers cast fearful and sus-picious glances over their shoulders at the castle as

Fifteen of his soldiers cruelly deserted him.

though they, too, firmly believed that the castellan of Pembroke was indeed a wizard.

So the castle was saved by Gerald's cunning, and soon the starving garrison was enjoying a well-earned feast provided by the Norman neighbours.

Some years later, King Henry became displeased with Earl Arnulf of Montgomery and took away his fortress. And he gave it to the worthy castellan, for, as the king agreed, the cunning defence of Gerald of Windsor had rightly won for him the Castle of Pembroke.

GEOFFREY EVANS

LUDLOW

In the middle ages barons waged war against each other and their castles changed hands in bewildering fashion.

4

A YOUNG PAGE PROVES HIS WORTH

A shrill peal of laughter rang through the courtyard of Ludlow Castle as a young page, engaged in a tilting contest, came tumbling in sorry fashion from his horse.

Again the laughter rang out as the horse cantered merrily away from him, refusing to be mounted again.

The page picked up his lance and looked angrily at a young girl whose merry voice hailed him, " Even your horse is ashamed of you, Fulk Fitz Warine ! See how he snorts in disgust."

Young Fulk turned sharply on his heel, but the girl Hawise ran lightly after him. " And is this how you show off your manners ! Remember, young sir, I am the daughter of the castle. Your father would not be pleased could he see you thus."

The boy's colour deepened as he remembered the morning his father had sent him to Ludlow Castle as a page to its lord, Jose de Dinan.

" You will enjoy a fine training, my son," his father

had said, " for you will have a chance in that noble household at Ludlow to train in knightly ways."

" A fine knight you will make ! " taunted the girl. " You had better descend to the kitchens and wield a ladle instead of a sword."

Young Fulk's ears burned. He longed to tell her she would soon repent of her words, but Hawise had already forgotten the incident and was loudly applauding a group of soldiers who were practising with the bow.

" I would that I could do some deed to prove my worth," muttered the page.

The opportunity came all too quickly, for early next morning, the loud cries of sentries awakened the sleeping garrison.

At the time of Stephen most men wore a split tunic and trousers of wool, bound with coloured straps.

" Enemies approach ! " cried one. "Rouse the soldiers!"

" They are Walter de Lacy's men ! " shouted another. " See his standard fly on the other bank of the Teme ! "

There was soon a lively scene in the courtyard as

33

the soldiers donned their armour, snatched their weapons and mounted their prancing steeds. Young Fulk, rubbing his eyes in the brilliant sunshine, caught sight of Hawise as she stood beside her father's waiting horse.

" Why does Lord de Lacy march against us ? " he asked.

" You should know that Walter de Lacy once lived here in Ludlow Castle," replied the maid. " But our King was displeased with him and granted the castle to my father. De Lacy now comes to fight for it again."

The page's eyes blazed with excitement, and as his master strode towards them he stepped eagerly forward.

" Do let me ride with you sire," he begged.

De Dinan laughed good naturedly. " I hear you cannot sit a horse properly yet. Nay, boy, you have much to learn before we send you to battle."

Fulk turned miserably from the emptying courtyard and did not see the sunlight glinting on the shields and helmets of the soldiers as they spurred their fresh horses through the gateway and down the hill towards the enemy.

" Come," cried Hawise, " do not look so sorrowful. Climb with me to the tower and watch the fray."

The ladies of the castle, their cloaks streaming in the wind on the tower top, were shouting words of encouragement as de Dinan's men drew nearer the enemy. So skilful were my lord's bowmen, and so swift and true did the arrows fly across the river, that soon de Lacy's soldiers were in slow retreat. Urging their horses onward, the soldiers of the garrison splashed across the river at its lowest point and soon the enemy were fleeing in all directions.

" Look ! " Hawise pointed to where her father was pursuing a running figure along the river bank. " It must be Walter de Lacy ! My father will capture him and bring him prisoner to the castle," she proudly added.

And, indeed, de Dinan had already overtaken the fugitive and overpowered him, for de Lacy was wounded. But as he dragged him from his horse, the onlookers from the tower beheld three of de Lacy's men, who had been hiding beneath the river bank, suddenly rush out. They encircled the lord of the castle and his captive.

Hawise turned in dismay to Fulk, but he had vanished. A few moments later, she saw a young horseman galloping recklessly down the hill towards the fray.

" It's Fulk Fitz Warine ! " The maid held her breath and watched.

Her father was weakened sadly, as with tired arms, he parried here and there to keep his enemies at bay. At any moment now he might come crashing from his steed.

Safely across the river, the young page raced to his master's aid. Raising his battleaxe aloft, he flung himself into the heart of the fray. De Lacy's men laughed at the young stripling who had ridden so fearlessly into their midst, but they soon found he was their match, and were amazed at the fury of his blows. They did not know that a girl's sharp words were rankling in his mind.

Grimly Fulk fought, turning and swerving so nimbly upon his horse that de Lacy's soldiers could not hem him in. And all the time he shielded his master, who, now too spent to fight, urged him on with weak cries.

So furious did the soldiers become as the young page evaded their blows, that they soon lost their tempers and wildly hit out at him.

"Will you let a stripling put you to shame!" gasped the wounded Walter de Lacy. "Beat him down I say, or you'll pay dearly for this."

Raising his battleaxe aloft, he flung himself into the heart of the fray.

Unheeding, young Fulk fought desperately on until two of de Lacy's men lay wounded on the grass. The third turned and fled for his life. By this time de Dinan's men, attracted by the cries, arrived upon the scene and heartily praised Fulk as they made Walter de Lacy their prisoner.

" You have saved my life ! " cried de Dinan to his page. " Here, take my sword for your own. I know it will remain in brave and worthy hands."

Delightedly Fulk took the sword, and· leading his master's horse, they slowly made their way towards the castle.

Long and clear rang the cheers of the ladies from the top of Ludlow's tower, but none rang more proudly than those of Hawise as she sped to greet the valiant page.

CARDIFF

G.E

Henry II (1154-1189) was King of England when William of Gloucester lived at Cardiff Castle. The powerful Norman earls often treated unfairly the Welsh chieftains who were their dependants.

5

THE REVENGE OF IVOR THE LITTLE

The costume of this time was plain in design, but of rich material and gaily coloured.

Down the steep mountain track a fine grey horse slowly picked its way. The rider jerked fitfully from side to side and seemed at a distance but a boy. However, a closer view would have told you that the owner of such a grim face, with black brows lowered, was no stripling, but a man. The rider was Ivor Bach, or Ivor the Little.

Over the summit of the mountain followed three other horsemen who dismounted and led their horses between the rough stones. Swinging round in his saddle, Ivor called out impatiently: " Ride ! Ride ! We'll never reach Cardiff Castle at this snail's pace."

And jerking at his horse's reins, he forced him into a gallop, and so amidst a cloud of dust the two went madly careering down the mountain path.

Ivor Bach was a Welsh Chieftain who owned a stretch of mountainous land called Senghenydd. Lately, he had suffered many insults from a neighbouring Norman lord. The little man determined to ride to Cardiff Castle and there seek audience and help from William, the powerful Earl of Gloucester.

At the castle, however, Ivor found no sympathy.

" You are a conquered people," said William, " and this is but your penalty."

What Ivor lacked in stature he made up in courage, and he fiercely replied, " Shame upon you for insulting a Chieftain of Wales ! "

At this outburst, the Earl commanded two of his soldiers to cast Ivor into one of the castle dungeons. " You will have time enough there to cool your fiery temper," he cried. And the struggling Ivor was roughly bundled into one of the gloomy dungeons, there to brood over the unfairness of his lot.

Some nights later, however, he was set free. As he waited for the drawbridge to be lowered, the soldiers sneered, " His Grace would have you set free at dead o' night. No doubt he hoped you would break that stubborn neck as you return to your wild mountains."

Ivor was about to reply, when some guests staying at the castle, called from the other side of the moat, that they wished to enter.

" The password ! " cried the soldier.

" Saint Fagan ! " came the reply.

" All's well ! " replied the other. " Enter ! "

" Saint Fagan ! " repeated Ivor softly as he hurried away from the castle. " I must not forget that password."

On arriving at his home, Ivor found that during his absence the Norman lord had robbed him of most of his land.

" We'll be driven from our homes, soon," cried one of Ivor's men. " then we'll have to live in the mountain caves."

" I wish that Earl William could taste of such discomforts," replied another.

" By my troth," cried Ivor suddenly, leaping to his feet, " I've a plan. We'll capture the Earl and bring him prisoner to one of our mountain caves."

" A fine plan, indeed," scoffed one. " Have you forgotten how impossible it is to break into Cardiff Castle ? "

" Besides," cried another, " have you forgotten the width of the great moat that encircles the castle ? Not to mention the high walls that are closely guarded."

" I have forgotten nothing," replied Ivor Bach.

That evening, after hurried preparations, the Welsh Chieftain and his men set off for Cardiff. Within sight of the castle, they tethered their horses in a copse and waited until it was well past midnight. Then, dropping on all fours, they crept towards the outer wall. They heard the clank of the sentry's footsteps as he marched to and from the gateway.

Suddenly, the sentry stopped and called out sharply, " Halt ! Who goes there ? " Luckily at that moment a frog croaked and hopped away. " Hm ! Scared by a frog, eh ! " muttered the sentry and continued his march.

Ivor and his men held their breath and crept along the wall to a spot where they were out of earshot. Then, each man unwound from about his body, a stout rope weighted at the end with a grappling hook. These were flung over the edge of the wall and the men were soon swarming up the ropes and over the wall.

" Now we must be bold," said Ivor. " We will march in a body towards the keep. In the gloom, the guard of the castle will think we are soldiers of the garrison."

The guard, in the gatehouse across the moat, saw them approach, but it was too dark to make out their forms. " They must be our men," he thought, " or

the sentry at the gate would have raised the alarm."
Then he rapped out, " Who goes there ? "

" Soldiers of the garrison," replied Ivor with a
trace of Norman accent.

" High time you were in," grumbled the guard.
" All the castle folk are asleep and I can't steal a solitary
wink. Hurry, give the password."

" Saint Fagan ! " came the prompt reply.

Immediately, the drawbridge was lowered and the
portcullis raised. Without delay, Ivor and his men
darted through, and before the guard realised he had
been tricked, he was overpowered. At point of the
sword, Ivor made him lead the way to the chamber
where Earl William slept. Fortunately for them, the
Earl was in a deep sleep after the feast of the previous
evening, and before he was properly awake, he found
himself gagged and bound and carried out of his castle.
Ivor swiftly gave orders that the Earl's wife and son
should be captured too, but he gave strict warning
that they should not be harmed, or unduly alarmed
by this sudden flight.

Not daring to risk the sentry's alarm, Ivor and his
men returned the way they had come, a number of
the strongest men hoisting the captives over the wall.

And when the hue and cry was raised, the Welshmen
were well on their way along secret paths that wound
into the mountains. The following days were spent

in mountain caves, and Earl William, listening to the wind as it moaned in the tree tops on the mountain edge, longingly thought of the great logs blazing merrily upon his castle hearth.

" I would take you to the warmth of my own fireside," mocked Ivor, " but your Norman lord has usurped my lands. From to-day this mountain cave is my home and, as you are my guest, you too must suffer these discomforts with me."

Realising by this time that his soldiers had failed to find the Welshmen's hiding place, Earl William promised Ivor that he would restore his lands if he could return with his wife and son to Cardiff Castle.

Willingly, Ivor agreed and the pact was settled. With great courtesy, the Welsh Chieftain accompanied his captives on their return, showing them the easiest paths and safest ways.

" Your bleak caves have made my castle dearer to me," cried Earl William. " Go, return to the valleys you love so well, and I give my word that no man shall dare punish you for what you have done."

And so, after friendly farewells, they parted company. That night, there was much merrymaking in the castle as Earl William related his adventure. But not one was happier than Ivor Bach as the wind blew and buffeted his small figure along the familiar paths that led to his home.

DYNEVOR

On many occasions during the 12th century the Welsh rulers refused to surrender their strongholds. One named Rhys ap Gruffydd, the lord of Dynevor Castle, was captured in battle and taken into England. Henry II despatched a Norman knight to explore the nature of the Welshman's lands.

THE FAITHFUL PRIEST
OF DYNEVOR

In the 12th century, the castle of Dynevor was the royal seat of the powerful Rulers of South Wales. Usually, it was a place of merriment and hospitality, for the rush strewn hall was filled with wandering musicians and bards who sang of the might and prowess of their fearless lord, Rhys ap Gruffydd. The courtyard, at dusk, usually echoed with the joyous cries of the lord and his company as they returned from hunting the wild stag over the moorland wastes and the tangled woods.

But soon the merry cries of the hunters were to turn to fierce cries of warfare, for Henry II of England was steadily marching through Wales forcing each Welsh ruler into subjection. For many years the intrepid Rhys had defied the King until he alone remained unconquered. One night, however, Rhys was taken by surprise, and was carried off into England before he could summon his soldiers.

The castle of Dynevor was silent and its lady sat weeping in her room that overlooked the peaceful

Towy while an old priest, the faithful Guaidanus, tried to comfort her.

The short cloak or mantle, worn at this time, is supposed to have been made popular by Henry II.

" My lord will never return," she sighed, " for King Henry has long tried to rid him of his power."

The old priest smiled. " There are means of restoring my lord to Dynevor. If my plan works well, not a single drop of blood will be spilled."

The lady looked up inquiringly. " But surely it is too late. Have we not received news that King Henry has sent a Breton Knight to take over the castle."

" Yes, but only if he is pleased with Dynevor and its surrounding country."

The lady gazed across at the verdant pastures rich with cattle and the dark forests where the wild beasts roamed and down to where the clear Towy abounded with fish. Sorrowfully, she said, " He will find this country all too pleasant I fear. But come," she added, " you must be on your journey. How ran the King's message ? "

" He bade me lead his Knight to Dynevor by the easiest route," replied the priest. Then he whispered with a chuckle, " He is still many days distant from the castle. I will conduct him by a route of my own."

The Breton Knight awaited him in a castle many miles away on the borders of Lord Rhys's country.

When the priest presented himself before the Knight, the latter cried impatiently, " If you journey so slothfully with me, I'll not need your company."

" As my lord pleases," replied Guaidanus, " but you will be wise to take me with you for I have discovered the easiest and most agreeable way to Dynevor."

So the party set out, the priest riding a little in front. Soon they came to a high mountain and as Guaidanus dismounted and started to lead his horse up the slope, the Knight exclaimed, " Must we needs climb this mountain when yonder path winds round the base of it ? "

" As my lord pleases," replied the priest, " but so many robbers and cut-throats infest that path, it is doubtful whether we should reach the other side alive."

With bad grace, the party dismounted, and unlike the priest who was accustomed to mountaineering, they soon showed signs of fatigue. When at last, with aching limbs, they reached a wood on the other side of the mountain, a halt was called. Wearily, the men

flung themselves upon the ground, too tired even to eat the food which they had brought with them.

To their amazement, however, Guaidanus began plucking grass and berries. When he had made a goodly pile of these together with rome roots and herbs, he sat before them and pretended to make a meal of them. Seeing the Knight's horrified face, the priest remarked, " We Welshmen often dine in this wise. It is our favourite food and no doubt in time you will acquire a taste for it." Peering around, he added in a low voice, " We had better be on our way for this wood is reputed to be inhabited by demons ! "

" Demons ! " exclaimed the Knight. He had often heard tales of weird happenings in the lonely valleys of Wales and here, in this silent wood, it was easy to believe them true. So, arising suddenly, he bade his men to be on their way, for he was anxious to reach the castle.

Once out of the wood, they were forced to dismount again because of the marshiness of the ground. Nervously they picked their way, their boots sinking and squelching amongst the green rushes. " If this is the easiest way to Dynevor," cried the Knight at last, "how could a stranger find his way there alone ? "

" He would never

Guaidanus dismounted and started to lead his horse up the slope.

reach the castle," replied the priest, "for he would probably sink in this treacherous bog."

Now the bog was simply the bed of a small stream, and Guaidanus knew that less than several yards away was a secure and dry pathway. But he had planned all this beforehand, forgetting his own discomfort in the enjoyment of the other's plight.

Reaching firmer ground, they decided to sleep there the night. But the Knight was too weary to sleep and seeing that the priest carried a small harp beneath his cloak, he commanded him to play.

And Guaidanus, perhaps thinking of his wronged master and the lonely Lady of Dynevor, played such a mournful air that it seemed as though the winds sighing in the trees on the mountain edge were in sympathy with him.

"Stop! Stop!" cried the Knight. "Do you not know any merry tunes?"

"Welshmen are never happier than when they are singing or playing plaintive music," replied the priest.

"Oh, I will never live with such people," cried the Knight. Already he longed to return to England to tell the King that he could never live among a race who were never happier than when they were sad, who lived on grass and wild roots and whose mountains sapped him of all his strength.

Guaidanus tried hard to conceal his delight when, after a few more days of similar journeying, the Knight was so discouraged that he bade him turn about and lead him out of Lord Rhys's country.

When King Henry heard the doleful report of his knight, he released Lord Rhys, having first made him swear oaths of loyalty to him. This my lord did, and gladly riding homewards, found the journey both good and pleasant especially when Guaidanus met him.

And as the two rode by singing streams through shady glens carpeted with springy grass, the green valley echoed with their laughter as the priest told his story.

Dynevor had already flung wide her gates and in the hall the musicians played merrily upon harp and pipe to welcome home the exiled lord and his faithful priest.

GEOFFREY EVANS.

FROM AN OLD PRINT.

ABERGAVENNY

William de Braose was one of the most powerful Norman barons in Wales in the 12th century. What he could not win by the sword he gained by treachery.

7

THE TREACHERY
OF WILLIAM DE BRAOSE

William de Braose rode swiftly over the frozen ground towards his castle. He had been riding from early morning through the sharp frosty air, but the sport had not put him in merry mood.

" My lord is pensive ? " One of his friends drew alongside the Norman knight. " Perhaps you tire of this castle of Abergavenny ? "

William de Braose shook his head. " It never looked fairer," he replied, as a bend in the road brought the castle into view. On all sides rose the gracious hills and the rounded top of one was capped with snow.

" Then my lord muses upon the strange guests he has invited to his castle to-night ? " persisted the other. " Indeed, the whole countryside talks of the feast. It will truly be an amazing sight to see Welshman and Norman sit peacefully together at their meat."

The Norman knight's brow darkened. In his heart he bitterly hated the Welsh people and their unyielding chieftains. Besides, hardly a year had passed since a Welshman had slain his uncle, Henry of Hereford.

These were troublous days when Norman and Welshman matched their wits against each other and castles were seized or surrendered so frequently that the cooks in their great kitchens ceased to bother their heads about their lord's favourite dish.

Henry II had of late summoned together a council of peace, and for a short while the bitter feuds came to an end.

Seemingly to celebrate this truce and under pretence of friendship, William de Braose had invited to his castle at Abergavenny a large number of Welsh chieftains. After much hesitation, the Welsh guests, led by Iorwerth of Caerleon, rode to Abergavenny to attend the feast.

" I hardly like the thought of sitting at a Norman's board ! " said one as they knocked at the castle gates.

" I do not trust this William de Braose," cried another. " I've heard too many tales of his cunning."

" We must forget all," cried Iorwerth cheerfully. "Come, what mood is this for a banquet ? If this

The minstrel would have certainly been trampled beneath the horses' hoofs.

Norman knight would show friendship towards us, then let us return it in good spirit."

" Have you forgotten so soon that it was a Norman sword that killed your son ? "

Iorwerth was about to reply when he noticed a lame minstrel slip and fall upon the frozen ground. At the same moment, the company of William de Braose came riding swiftly towards him. The minstrel would have certainly been trampled beneath the horses' hoofs had not Iorwerth leaped to his aid and snatched him from danger.

The lame minstrel's eyes were filled with gratitude as he cried, " Perhaps Roderic the Minstrel will soon repay you for this." Iorwerth laughed and dropped a silver coin into the minstrel's shabby pouch. Then, forgetting the incident, he proceeded with the others into the castle.

The tables in the banqueting hall creaked and groaned with roasted ox and fowl, with fish and venison, and the silver-rimmed horns were filled to the brim with fresh mead. The Welsh chieftains forgot their doubts and misgivings, and were soon in high spirits.

" For I trow," cried one Welsh chieftain, " this Wales of ours is so fair to gaze upon that it would be sinful if we did not share its beauty with other eyes."

Meanwhile, the brow of William de Braose grew darker and it was remarked by those who sat near him that he ate little. The sharp eyes, however, of the lame minstrel who played softly upon the harp noticed all this, and more besides, and he slowly edged his way towards the place where Iorwerth sat.

Bending close, he whispered, " An evil plot lurks behind de Braose's brow. Look to your sword."

Hardly had he uttered the warning than the Norman knight leaped to his feet. " Silence ! " he cried.

The laughter died away as all gazed at his sullen face, yet none of the Welshmen suspected the evil deed that was about to be done.

" It is pleasant, indeed," he began, " that Norman and Welshman are at peace, but since we are the victors, I must enforce this rule : From this day forth no Welshman must carry arms, either sword or bow. I command every Welshman present to swear an oath to obey my order."

With one accord, the Welshmen indignantly shouted their disapproval.

" This is an injustice ! " cried one.

" We are betrayed ! " shouted another. " This feast was but a trick ! To take away our arms is to deprive us of our rights ! "

Hotly protesting, the Welshmen rose to depart, but swiftly the false de Braose gave a signal, and from behind the heavy tapestries and from secret hiding places rushed armed Norman soldiers, their swords bared as they beat down the bewildered captives.

But because of the minstrel's warning, Iorwerth was prepared. He had already drawn his sword, and now fighting manfully, parrying the Norman thrusts this way and that, he escaped from the dreadful scene. So outnumbered were the trapped chieftains, that all except Iorwerth were ruthlessly slain.

When Iorwerth told the tale of this terrible massacre, large forces of Welsh troops, eager for revenge, rallied around him. Seven years passed, however, before the death of their countrymen was avenged. Then dawn, breaking over the hills of Abergavenny, beheld a smouldering ruin where once had stood a proud Norman castle.

GEOFFREY EVANS

HAVERFORDWEST

Robbers and thieves roamed the mountains and valleys of Wales during the 12th century. Taking advantage of the unsettled times, they plundered and robbed. Once caught and cast into a castle dungeon, there was little hope of escape.

THE OUTLAW ARROW MAKER
OF HAVERFORDWEST

The sun, slanting through a beech tree, cast a pattern of lace upon the green jerkins of five young archers as they silently sharpened their arrows outside the walls of Haverfordwest castle.

Three of the boys were the sons of the Earl of Pembroke and the other two the sturdy sons of the lord of the castle. Hugh, the eldest, had cut a crude circle in the bark of an oak some distance away and this was their target.

" Ready ? " he cried.

The boys nodded and, with nimble fingers, each carefully fitted his arrow to the bow. Each boy was secretly confident that his arrow alone would remain quivering in the heart of the distant target.

Ping! Hugh's arrow sped from its taut bow. There was a quick intake of breath as the arrow bravely hit the target, then a dismayed gasp as it dropped bluntly to the ground. In quick succession, the other arrows sped towards their mark, but each one followed the fate of the first and lay in the bracken below.

" The arrowheads are blunt. That's the trouble," sighed young John.

" And mine took all the morning to make," grumbled Hugh, but his face brightened as he pointed to some horsemen galloping with all speed towards the castle. The boys raced to the castle gates and were rewarded by the sight of a ruffianly looking fellow being flung from his horse and dragged into the courtyard.

He pointed to some horsemen galloping fiercely towards the castle.

" He's the Chief of the Outlaws ! " shouted one of the soldiers. " We caught him in a copse some miles away."

The boys hopped this way and that to snatch a closer view of the notorious captive, who was struggling in vain to free himself.

" He was sleeping so sweetly, it was a sin to rouse him, eh ? " guffawed another. " My lord will be pleased. He's a dangerous bandit and is said to be the finest archer in these parts."

" Give him a bow and arrows and he's as safe as a fox in his lair," added a third.

The boys gazed admiringly at the robber's tattered clothes and grisly face, and following close at the heels of the soldiers, went down the narrow twisting steps that led to the dark dungeon beneath. Growling and threatening vengeance, the outlaw was, at length, securely locked in his prison. Old Amos, the goaler, hitched the heavy key to his great belt and sat as sentry on a bench near by.

" Aye," he muttered as the robber violently beat his great fists against the iron studded door, " you can hammer away if it pleases you, but it is you who will break down first."

After a while, the hammering and threatening

The gown of this time was quite loose, with a deep band round the neck and round the hem of the skirt, which was very full.

died away and Old Amos's head sank in slumber.

Young John picked up a half-burnt torch which had been dropped in the struggle and the boys tip-toed past Old Amos and peered through the iron grating in the dungeon door.

" Hist ! " whispered Hugh, " is it true you're a fine archer ? "

The robber growled, then flattened his coarse face against the grating. " Pish ! And much good it brings me now."

" Can you make good arrows ? " Young John thrust his arrow between the bars—" better than this one ? "

" Pah ! " spat the robber. " This isn't an arrow ! Here, give me your knife. Those rogues have taken my dagger."

Hugh eagerly thrust his knife between the bars while John held the torch close to the opening. With deft strokes the bandit cut at the arrow, and soon he was boasting of his reckless deeds; of the strength that lay in the big muscles of his brown arms, and of the wealthy travellers he had robbed in lonely valleys.

The boys listened with rapt attention, and when the arrow was pushed back through the grating, they were loth to leave the musty gloom of the dungeon that held captive so doughty and fearless a bandit.

The arrow proved to be a great success and day after day the boys, hiding a tasty joint or half-eaten fowl beneath their jerkins—for the robber had a ravenous appetite—stole down to the dungeon, to return with their quivers bristling with newly-cut arrows.

Of late, Old Amos had been bribed and persuaded to let the boys into the dungeon, and, under the expert teaching of the prisoner, they were soon able to make fine arrows that not only sped truly to the mark, but, having pierced the target, lay proudly quivering in its heart. But the outlaw became restless and longed for the freedom and excitement of his former life.

" Besides," he confided to the boys, " my hands are growing tender and losing their cunning. I vow even my sharp eyes have lost their keenness in this gloom."

One noon, the boys conspired to secure their arrow-maker his freedom. The sleeping Amos had un-wittingly left the dungeon-key in its lock while the boys were paying their usual visit. The door was left

The lord implored the outlaw to spare the boys.

slightly ajar, and it would have been an easy matter for the robber to have stolen out. But the boys knew that two stalwart soldiers kept guard at the entrance above and that they would soon raise the alarm.

Hugh softly drew the key from the lock and fitted it on the inside of the door. The boys slipped into the dungeon and secured the door behind them. With a creak and a groan the key was slowly turned.

" Here, take the key," whispered Hugh to the outlaw, " for now we are your prisoners ! Pretend you will slay us if our father does not set you free."

With one accord the boys set up such realistic cries

of terror that Old Amos awoke with a start. With the bandit's threats echoing in his ears, he hobbled away, calling to the lord and his men that the wily bandit, having enticed the boys into the dungeon, was now about to put them to death.

Soon, the dark crannies of the dungeon were lit up with the flaring torches of the soldiers as the lord implored the outlaw to spare the boys.

" Set me free and I'll not harm them," growled the outlaw.

Only too willingly, the request was granted and, as the soldiers grimly lowered their swords and stepped aside, the robber sauntered up the twisting stairway. Once clear of the castle gates, he swiftly took to his heels.

Perhaps the boys had arranged a trysting place beyond the castle walls, for it was strange that later they became so skilful with the bow that their expert archery would have done credit event to the Outlaw himself.

RECONSTRUCTED FROM AN OLD PRINT.

BUILTH

GEOFFREY EVANS

Edward I (1272-1307) desired to unite England and Wales under one rule. At the same time, Llewelyn, last of the Welsh Princes, fought for the freedom of Wales.

9

THE BETRAYAL OF
LLEWELYN THE LAST

A heavy mantle of snow covered the hills and dales far beyond the castle of Builth. Some miles distant, a small force of Welsh soldiers huddled around their camp fires. Apart from them sat their beloved Prince, Llewelyn ap Gruffydd, and his faithful squire, Grono.

" Yonder lies the road to Builth Castle," said Grono, pointing to a rough road that led into the gloom.

" We will march there to-morrow," replied the Welsh Prince. " The king's men follow so hotly upon our heels, that we must plan to rejoin our allies without delay."

" We can thank Welsh traitors for betraying our hiding places." Grono drew closer to his prince. " But do you think we can trust this John Giffard, Keeper of Builth Castle ? I hear he is in league already with our enemy Edmund Mortimer."

Llewelyn was silent. So many rumours and evil tales had reached his ears during the past treacherous months, when Edward had pitilessly hounded him

To protect their legs men wore bandages of twisted straw.

through his native mountains, that it was hard to know who were his true friends. Having left his army in the mountains, he had come with a small bodyguard to put new heart into his supporters.

" Giffard has given me word that the castle shall be ours," he said at length. " I dare not think otherwise, for then all our hopes are lost."

Suddenly, there was a shout from one of the sentries as a strange horseman came riding with all haste along the road.

Flinging himself before the Welsh Prince, he said in a low voice, " I bring good news, O Prince ! A number of Welsh chieftains bade me tell you that they wish to meet you to-night at Aberedw. There they will plan with you a rising against Edward. But they implore you to ride alone so that you will not attract the attention of the English spies."

Llewelyn's face brightened. " The first cheerful news I have received for many weary months," he cried.

"Aberedw lies a few miles down the Wye," exclaimed Grono. "There lives a blacksmith named Red Madoc o' the Wide Mouth."

Further begging Llewelyn to ride alone, the messenger leaped upon his horse and rode into the night.

When Llewelyn and his faithful squire arrived at Aberedw a little before midnight, something in the eeriness of the lonely spot made them doubt the truth of the secret message.

"I feel this is a plot to capture you unguarded," said Grono, fearfully peering around. "Come, let us return with all haste to our camp."

Llewelyn pointed to the imprint of their horses' shoes in the snow.

"They will follow our track," he replied, then added swiftly, "Where lives this blacksmith, Red Madoc?"

Grono pointed to a cottage ahead of them and Llewelyn spurred his horse forward. Bursting into the smithy, he commanded Red Madoc to take off their horse's shoes and nail them on backwards.

Not recognising the Welsh Prince in the gloom, the smith exclaimed, "Backwards! You are crazy!"

But as a golden coin was pressed into his hand, he quickly set about the task and soon Llewelyn and Grono were riding with difficulty from Aberedw.

Thinking of the track they made in the snow, Grono chuckled, " Now all our steps lead to the smithy and not one leads from it."

Seeing a number of torches in the distance moving in their direction, the two hid in a nearby cave to watch the horsemen pass.

" We will soon find out whether our doubts are true," whispered Llewelyn.

Flinging himself before the Welsh Prince, he said in a low voice, " I bring good news, O Prince."

As the soldiers came riding by, they could see that their leader was Mortimer, one of their bitterest enemies.

That night, the two hid in the cave while Mortimer's men awaited their arrival at Aberedw. At early dawn, they stole from their hiding-place, and joining their small force of soldiers, rode swiftly towards the castle of Builth.

By this time Mortimer's men, having forced Red Madoc to relate the Welshman's trick, rode fiercely in pursuit.

As the brave Welsh soldiers crossed the narrow wooden bridge over the Wye, they could hear the shouts of the enemy close at hand.

" Hew down the bridge ! " shouted Llewelyn, and as the first Englishman reined in his horse on the opposite bank, the bridge crashed into the swollen river.

" Ride for your lives to the castle ! " cried Llewelyn. " We will be safe there for a while."

A sigh of relief escaped from their lips as the grey walls of the castle loomed into view. Eagerly and loudly Llewelyn knocked upon the castle gates, but no welcoming shout answered. The gates remained locked against them.

" Open in the name of your Prince ! " commanded Llewelyn.

Then came the dreaded reply from within : " We have no Prince ; Edward is our King ! "

" Where is your master, John Giffard ? " shouted the young squire. " He promised the castle should be ours."

"John Giffard rides with Edmund Mortimer," was the curt answer.

Desperate, Llewelyn turned away, and beckoning his faithful men, rode slowly from the castle. " Come," he cried bravely, " we still have courage enough to fight a thousand traitors."

" Llewelyn to the last ! " shouted his men, each one eager to lay down his life for the dauntless prince.

But the uneven struggle was soon to end.

Next day, the English, in powerful numbers poured down upon the fearless Welsh soldiers and slew them at their post. And in a gorse-covered dingle above the waters of the Irfon, Llewelyn the Last was slain by a soldier named Adam de Frankton.

That night, John Giffard, returning to his castle, found it hard to forget that noble and gallant prince who had so cruelly been turned away from its gates.

GEOFFREY EVANS.

CAERNARVON

After Llewelyn's death, the Welsh demanded a Prince of their own. Edward I conferred the title of " Prince of Wales " upon his son, a title which the eldest sons of the Kings of England have since borne.

10

THE INFANT PRINCE
OF WALES

Six young heralds, their surcoats emblazoned with the Royal arms, marched in line down the steps of Queen Eleanor's Gate. With a flourish the long silver trumpets were raised to their lips and a brave fanfare echoed throughout the castel of Caernarvon and beyond.

" The King is coming ! "

There was a low hubbub of voices and the ladies in vivid-hued dresses of scarlet and green and blue raised their mantles in readiness to curtsy. Their wimples of snowy whiteness, draped carefully around their eager faces, bobbed and nodded as they whispered to each other. They did not heed the foolish antics of a jester as he darted from one to another, impudently jingling his merry bells beneath their noses.

Their bright eyes were fixed upon the gateway for they dare not miss any of the ceremony that was about to take place. Had not Queen Eleanor bade them watch close and report to her every detail of the scene ?

A lady pointed to a band of grim Welsh chieftains who stood apart from the others

Then triumphantly turning towards the chieftains he offered them his son.

" Our King has summoned them here. He has promised to give them a prince of their own."

Indeed, the chieftains had come at Edward's bidding, but in their hearts they did not trust him. Had not Edward's men slain their own beloved Llewelyn, last of the native princes of Wales ? In the mountain caves and fastnesses dark plots were hatched against English foes. Welshmen, longing for freedom and liberty, demanded a prince of their own.

" I'll give you a prince ! " Edward had promised the Welsh chieftains. " I'll give you a son of Wales who cannot speak an English word ; a worthy prince whose life is pure and whose honour bears no stain."

And the Welsh warriors, half believing, half doubting, came to Caernarvon to see the fulfilment of Edward's promise.

Meanwhile, the throng below the gateway had increased. A small crowd of Welsh peasants with their dark-eyed children came curiously to watch what the great monarch would do. A band of blackgarbed monks and nuns in white raiment mingled with the people. Far-travelled pilgrims rested awhile ; and a troupe of wandering minstrels joined the company.

Swiftly the tale had spread of Edward's promise. What a tale to tell and sing in castle hall or grey cloistered monastery!

An aged bard plucked at the strings of his harp and his sweet-voiced boy poured out a song of the sadness of Wales.

" The King! "

The men in mail, posted at the gate stood rigidly to attention.

The trumpets sounded and proudly the tall figure of the warrior King appeared. His standard bearers strode before, his grey-haired counsellors walked close upon their king.

Suspiciously, the Welsh chieftains waited. In vain they looked for a prince at Edward's side, but the King stood out alone.

" He has failed us! He brings no prince! "

A wave of unrest swept over them as impatiently they watched with darkening brows.

But once more the young heralds proudly raised their silver trumpets, and this time the fanfare came soft and low, for down the steps towards the King, with slow, dignified tread, stepped a nursing woman and her handmaidens.

In the nursing woman's arms lay a small white bundle!

A tense hush fell upon the waiting company. The Welsh warriors were puzzled. The sun caught the glint of a strong mailed arm as the soldierly Edward raised the tiny babe and laid him gently upon his shield.

Then triumphantly turning towards the chieftains he offered them his son.

" Behold ! your Prince ! "

The amazement of the Welshmen changed to delight as they gazed upon the infant prince. Here, indeed, lay a true son of Wales, one born within Caernarvon's walls Eagerly they knelt before him, their enmity and bitterness forgotten as with proud beating hearts they paid homage to their prince.

And Edward, remembering the fierceness of these Welsh warriors in past warfare, smiled upon his son.

In the reign of Edward the First, coats were loose with a hood attached.

Satisfied, the Welsh chieftains journeyed homewards and spread the glad news in hamlet and vale. The story of grim Edward's joke was retold in castle hall and in humble cottage. One and all, however, rejoiced over the gift of the babe who was to be known as the " First Prince of Wales."

Not even the bards or aged seers could foretell the future of this infant prince. Little then did they dream that one day when the babe had grown up and had become Edward II, King of England, he would return to his native land, not with pomp and celebration, but furtively and secretly and all he asked of the Welsh people was a hiding place.

GEOFFREY EVANS

CAERPHILLY

Edward II (1307-1327) was fond of pomp and gaiety. His courtiers repeatedly offended the hard-fighting barons. After a reign of failure, Edward was deposed and he fled to Wales.

A FUGITIVE KING IN PEASANT'S CLOTHES

A waggon groaned and rumbled along the highway that led to Caerphilly. The merchant driver reined in his horses as he came upon a peasant stumbling along carrying a sack bulging with loaves of bread.

" Hola ! " cried the merchant. " Is this the way to the castle ? "

" Yes," shouted the peasant, " and it's hard walking between these ruts. From early morning there's been a long string o' laden carts and waggons all making their way to the castle. The King and his men must be right hearty fellows, for I've not seen so much meat

A fashionably dressed man of the 14th century. The long sleeved outer garment was called a Houppelande.

and corn and fish in all my life. My wife has just baked these loaves for the King."

" You may as well ride along with me, then," replied the merchant, making room for the peasant to climb into his waggon. As the other settled himself, he whispered, " Have you seen the King ? "

The peasant shook his head. " No, but if tales run true he has an idle, foolish head upon his shoulders."

The merchant laughed. " And mighty foolish, too, if he cannot hold his own wife in check. Why, I heard news this morning that Queen Isabella and her son are pursuing him with a vast army ! "

The peasant's eyes widened. " First the King and now the Queen ! In truth, Caerphilly will be famous ! Well, I hope they keep their fighting within the castle." He looked warily from side to side, then added slowly, " Mark my words, there's only one fellow at the root o' this present evil, and he's Hugh le Despenser, Lord o' the Castle. The King could do no greater folly than trust to him."

Finding himself without an army, the King had been forced to flee for his life, and so he had journeyed to Caerphilly, the home of his favourite, there hoping to find shelter within the gigantic battlements of the castle.

On arrival at the castle, Edward had sent out messengers into the outlying districts bidding all merchants bring him provisions.

The peasant pointed to the far-stretching pastures that lay around. " There's not a single cow or sheep left alive in these parts," he said. " They've all been slaughtered at the King's command ; —and salt! Why, only this morning a soldier of the garrison told me there's enough salt come from Bristol to fill up one of the castle towers ! "

" Ho, ho," laughed the merchant. " then he'll be right glad of my barrels here filled with good ale, eh ? Indeed the King is determined he will not be starved into surrendering."

And so the waggon clumsily creaked on its way towards the castle wherein the King of England was a fugitive.

The King was in despair, for each hour brought word that one Welsh chieftain after another refused commands to give him support. He turned angrily upon his favourite, Hugh le Despenser. " I see you have so made Caerphilly the seat of your base intrigues that not one Welsh lord will send his soldiers here."

Never at a loss for escaping a difficulty, Hugh replied quickly, " If we cannot summon these men, my liege, why not grant freedom to all murderers and thieves in prison—on condition that they fight for you!"

"Better a motley army of rebels and traitors, than not one at all," said the King, bitterly.

And the two hurried from the court, where the raw November fog lingered, into the Royal apartments, there to prepare the command. But it was already too late, for at that moment a messenger breathlessly burst into the King's presence.

"O, my liege," he cried, flinging himself at Edward's feet, "I bear dread news! Queen Isabella and your son press this way!"

The King buried his head in his hands. "So soon!" he muttered. "So ruthlessly am I hounded, they will not let me rest a single night."

Even Hugh le Despenser's face was white as he cried, "And the Queen's forces?"

"Alack! Thousands strong!" replied the messenger. "They are now only a few miles distant."

The King leaped to his feet. "Come, we must be gone. I'll not tarry here."

Hugh caught at the King's arm. "You forget this castle is impregnable. Do you not remember praising its mighty defences? We are securely hidden here, not within one castle, but three!"

"They'll find a way in!" cried the King. "If

their battering rams fail to break down the walls their hatred of me will so aid their cunning that they will rout me out. I'll flee while there is yet time."

" But all will recognise you! I beg you, my liege, stay here," implored Hugh.

" I'll disguise myself," went on the King, unheeding; " now what best apparel to wear! "

At this the messenger stepped forward. " And it please my liege, there's a merchant with barrels of ale and a peasant with loaves of bread waiting in the outer courtyard."

" Then bring the peasant to me! " commanded the King.

The King unclasped his cloak and kicked off his

long pointed shoes as the trembling peasant was brought before him.

" I only brought loaves for the King," cringed the peasant, as the bulging sack toppled over and the loaves came tumbling merrily out.

" And little thought you would lay them right at the King's feet! Come," cried Edward impatiently, " off with your tunic and clumsy shoes."

With shaking fingers, the peasant handed his shabby hooded cloak to the King. Edward flung it over his shoulders and pulled the peaked hood well over his face. " I am now indeed rid of the last traces of my royal dignity," he murmured.

So, as the thick November fog closed in upon Caerphilly Castle, a bewildered peasant slowly dropped to the floor a richly embroidered royal cloak, while its fugitive owner, clad in rough homespun, stole by secret paths to yet another hiding-place.

FROM AN OLD PRINT.

F L I N T

Richard II (1377-1399) *had unfairly banished his cousin Henry Bolingbroke from the realm. This and many other acts of injustice made the king very unpopular with his people. On Richard's return from Ireland he found Henry's forces too strong and he escaped in disguise to North Wales.*

12

THE KING'S HOUND ALTERS A DYNASTY

Richard II, King of England, sat alone in one of the rooms of Flint Castle. The walls were hung with pennons and shields bearing the Royal arms, but there was no grandeur here or display of finery.

A page timidly entered leading by the hand a blind harpist.

" Sire," said the page nervously, for he feared the King's violent spirit, " this man claims to be a soothsayer. He is the only one I could find living near the castle."

" Leave us alone ! " The King arose and immediately a lithe hound sprange gracefully after him. " Nay Mathe," cried Richard in gentler tone, bending to smooth the dog's sleek head, "I did not wish that you, too, should go. Come, since I have no other loyal friend in this bleak castle, you shall be my counsellor."

He crossed to a window seat and gazed out into the gathering dusk, while Mathe, pushing his cold nose into his master's hand, looked up at him with a wealth of affection.

The blind bard plucked softly at the strings of his harp. " Let my music first soothe you, my liege," he cried, " for I feel you are restless and ill at ease."

" No," Richard spoke impatiently. " If your music is as gloomy as your brooding Welsh mountains, I'll not hear it. Come, soothsayer," he said in troubled tone, " what do you foretell for your King? Forget I am the King and speak openly."

" Men say that Richard of England was slain in Irish soil."

Richard stamped his foot. " So this is their evil plot to rid me of my throne! This is the reason my men fled when I landed on Welsh soil! What traitor's work is this? "

The bard gazed before him with steady, unseeing eyes. " All men now flock to one who was unjustly banished from England. Thousands rally around him as he returns to claim the land that you so cruelly snatched from him."

" Not my cousin, Harry Bolingbroke! " cried Richard. " He has not dared return against me?"

" He returns to rid England of the base

Richard leapt to the window and in the light of a hundred torches he could see a strong body of soldiers led by a mailed figure.

flatterers that infest the realm. He returns to right the countless wrongs that for twenty weary years Richard wrought unto his people ! "

" Stop ! Stop ! " The King's face was livid. " Would you thus upbraid your monarch ? "

The bard answered, " My liege bade me forget he was the King."

" Aye," rejoined Richard bitterly, " an easy matter to forget I am the King. It is mockery to address me so. Where are the loyal subjects that should protect me now ? Where are the vast forces that should guard our realm against ambitious traitors ? Where is the pomp and glory that should now attend me ? I have none ! "

Suddenly his mood changed and he said softly, " Come, play your harp now. Let me hear your most mournful music, then it shall be in keeping with Richard's spirit."

And so the blind bard lovingly plucked the strings of his harp, and for all the sadness and woe that poured from them, Richard's sorrow was deeper.

Softly the page entered, carrying long candles and these he placed in the sconces on either side the hearth so that their flickering flames lit up the troubled face of the King.

As the music died away, Richard caressed his hound's

head. " I said I had no loyal friend. Forgive me Mathe, for you are so faithful a subject you will not let me move a single pace but that you are guarding close at my heels."

The soothsayer arose. " Mark my words, O sire," he said on departing. " As long as the hound is faithful, you need not fear losing your crown. For every hound knows a rightful master."

" Then," cried Richard with forced gaiety, " since Mathe will never leave my side, I know I shall always keep my crown."

The soothsayer went his way and Richard thought deeply of what he had prophesied. Suddenly there came a blaring trumpet note from without the castle walls. Richard leapt to the window and in the light of a hundred torches he could see a strong body of soldiers led by a mailed figure.

" My cousin, Bolingbroke ! "

A few minutes later Bolingbroke entered the King's room. He was fully armed and carried his helmet in the crook of his arm. Walking

Towards the end of Richard the Second's reign, women's dress became more sombre.

95

swiftly to where Richard stood he knelt before him.

" My liege," he cried, " Harry Bolingbroke, in bringing allegiance to his King, craves the return of his lands."

" They are restored to you, fair cousin," replied Richard, then forcing a smile he bade the newcomer arise. " For if all rumours run true, it is I who should be kneeling before you," he said.

As he spoke, Mathe left the King's side and restlessly paced from one to the other.

" And now my mission," cried Bolingbroke arising. " The commons bade me come to you. They say you have ruled them ill for twenty years, and have sent me to help you govern them with wiser laws."

Richard fingered his hound's silken ears, but Mathe, with surprising suddenness, shook itself free.

" Come here, Mathe," the King commanded. Obediently the dog returned to Richard's side, but as he caressed it, once again Mathe sidled away.

Crossing to Bolingbroke, the hound at length raised its front paws so that they rested on his arm, and, wagging its tail, fawned upon him.

" Mathe ! " the King called for the last time, but unheeding, the dog sought Bolingbroke's hand as though it wished to be caressed. As the soothsayer's words flashed into his mind, Richard murmured sadly, " My whole realm has turned against me, but the loss of Mathe is the hardest to bear."

The dog dropped lightly to its feet and contentedly walked around Bolingbroke, brushing its sleek head against his mailed suit, then finally curled itself around its new master's feet.

" Cousin Harry ! cried Richard. " Behold ! From this moment you are King of England. For every hound knows a rightful master ! "

And, with a puzzled frown, Bolingbroke stared down upon the sleeping hound as, brokenly, Richard turned away.

HARLECH

During the Wars of the Roses, the Houses of York and Lancaster fought over the English throne. In the 15th century the West of Wales stood out for Lancaster. Although a Yorkist King, Edward IV, was crowned, still Harlech remained Lancastrian.

13

WHEN HARLECH CASTLE WAS BESIEGED

There was a rattle of falling stones as some unseen figures leaped across the craggy boulders on the mountain slope.

The tired troop of English horsemen, riding along the narrow path below, glanced fearfully up. But the spies had vanished into the grey mist.

" Is any country so desolate as these mountain fastnesses ? " muttered one of the riders.

" Better keep a sharp look-out," warned another, " or we may not escape a falling boulder as luckily as we did the last one."

Behind the horsemen stumbled a never ending line of Yorkist soldiers. It was deep winter, and as the men came upon snowdrifts that blocked the mountain passes, they were forced to wait while their Welsh guides cut rough pathways through the frozen snow. The wind shrieked and howled about their ears, and sudden bursts of icy hail beat upon them.

" I vow the wind and hail are in league with this Welsh traitor at Harlech," cried one of the horsemen whose face ached from the stinging hail. Then, looking up at the gloomy mountains that frowned on either side, he added, " Dafydd ap Jevan is welcome to his country. It's a land o' demons ! "

" You change your feelings swiftly then for a Yorkist ! " rebuked his companion. " Only an hour ago you longed to be at Harlech to rout the Welsh traitor out of his craggy lair. Think of it, he is the only Lancastrian left that holds out against the King ! "

" Yes, and for almost eight years now he has resisted us," said another. " I wonder King Edward is not weary of sending us year after year to Harlech. Besides, the castle is so strongly built that only a wizard could get into it."

Thus it was that after the Wars of the Roses, a petty Welsh chieftain openly defied King Edward IV. In a final effort to conquer him, Edward had mustered his strongest forces under the command of a fierce fighter and brave leader named Sir Richard Herbert.

" I'll make this traitor surrender or die in the attempt," vowed Sir Richard as he set off to Wales with his army.

So after terrible hardships amidst the bleak Welsh mountains, the Yorkists reached the stern fortress of

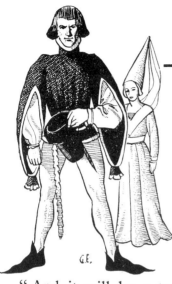

Harlech that overlooked the grey sea. Breathlessly, the men watched Sir Richard's messenger climb the steep ascent to the castle, the white flag of truce in his hand.

" Harlech is a crag built upon a crag ! " said one of the soldiers.

" And it will be a tough nut to crack ! " replied another, " especially if all we hear of this Welsh chieftain is true. I hear he is a mightily built man."

" And so he should be, "rejoined another, " for no one but a giant would live in such forbidding country."

By this time, the messenger had reached the castle, and, blowing upon his trumpet, he commanded in the King's name that the Welsh chieftain should surrender the castle of Harlech. A hush fell upon the Yorkists as the massive figure of Dafydd ap Jevan appeared upon the battlements. Sweeping his eyes over the immense forces of the English below, he called out in a fearless voice, " Go, tell your King I once held a castle in

France until all the old women of Wales talked of it. I will now hold this castle in Wales until all the old women of France gossip about it."

At such a flaunting challenge, Sir Richard gave the signal for immediate attack and the siege began. With grim determination, the English placed their long ladders against the castle walls in their attempts to scale them, but they were repeatedly flung back by the sturdy men of Harlech.

Stones and missiles were sent hurtling against the towers, and the Yorkist arrows flew thick and fast. Sir Richard used every means to make a breach in the great walls, but all his efforts were in vain. Harlech remained as immovable as the rock upon which it stood.

Meanwhile, inside the castle, the burly chieftain and his one hundred brave soldiers realised that such

In a flash, a number of Welshmen leaped upon Sir Richard and dragged him into the castle.

a siege could not last for ever. So that night, Dafydd secretly sent out a number of his finest archers to hide in the mountains above the castle.

Next day the fighting continued. Urging his men, Sir Richard again led them up the slope towards the castle gates. But, to their dismay, a sudden storm of arrows poured down upon them from the mountain behind. The Yorkists fled here and there in all directions and, in the confusion, Sir Richard reached the gateway alone. To his amazement, the great iron gates slowly opened before him.

" Seize him ! "

In a flash, a number of Welshmen leaped upon Sir Richard and dragged him into the castle. Hearing his shouts, the Yorkists rushed to the spot, but the great gates had shut, imprisoning their brave leader, who still fought to free himself.

In vain, the Yorkists battered upon the gateway, calling down threats upon the Welshmen's heads for this outrageous trick, but no sound came from within Harlech's walls, and the soldiers turned away in dismay.

They imagined he would be made to suffer untold tortures from the hands of the giant Welshman, but had they been able to peep into the banqueting hall of Harlech that night, they would have beheld a very different scene.

The former enemies were merrily feasting together, and so much did the one admire the prowess of the other, that the two soon became firm friends.

"I'll give you yet another chance to capture Harlech," sportingly offered Dafydd. "You shall be set free at dawn."

Sir Richard shook his head. "No, I cannot again fight one who has treated me so nobly. And yet," Sir Richard frowned, "I vowed to the King I would either make you surrender or die in the attempt. There is nothing left then but that you must put me to death and let my men carry on with the siege."

Dafydd replied slowly, "For eight years I have kept the English King at bay. Do you think, if I yielded for your sake he would grant me my life and freedom?"

Sir Richard took the Welsh chieftain's hand in his own. "I'll guard your life with my own, and the King, I promise, will grant you your freedom."

So the long siege of Harlech ended. Sir Richard kept his vow, for although King Edward bitterly hated the Welsh chieftain, who had for so many years defied him, yet he granted Dafydd his life and liberty.

It was many years before the Yorkist soldiers forgot that hard winter in Wales, or the burly chieftain who dwelt in the craggy fortress that stood between the mountains and the grey sea.

GEOFFREY EVANS.

CAREW

Sir Rhys ap Thomas, lord of Carew Castle, had helped to place Henry Tudor on the throne. Many honours were bestowed upon the aged knight and to celebrate these he held a vast entertainment at Carew Castle.

14

THE FEAST OF A THOUSAND GUESTS

Long before the break of dawn, the household of Carew Castle was astir.

Simplicity was the keynote of women's dress in the early sixteenth century.

Woodmen, with gleaming axes, hewed great logs in readiness for the kitchen fires. Maidens hung the rich tapestries in the halls and gently shook out the folds so that the scenes of the Crusades, or of the tournament, seemed to awaken into sudden life.

The castle soldiers polished their armour so that they could see their faces mirrored therein. In one of the tower rooms a lady smoothed out her finest dress, deftly adding a stitch here and there to secure a velvet ribbon.

Even the bards, hidden away in a little room at the far end of the castle, practised upon their harps in readiness for the day's festivities. What were they playing? One sang of Sir Rhys ap Thomas, the lord of the castle, and of his noble life. Another sang of

the banquet that was to be held that day.

A minstrel, watching the first streak of dawn breaking into light, sang that his dream was now fulfilled, for Henry Tudor, a Welsh-born King, reigned upon the English throne.

Away beyond the hustle and bustle of the castle walked young Griffith ap Rhys, my lord's son. After him, the hem of her flowing gown wet from the dew, ran a little girl.

" Why, Luned ! " cried the boy, " how did you persuade your nursing maid to let you out so early ! "

" She needed little persuasion," replied Luned roguishly. " She was snoring so loudly she did not hear me steal from the room. Indeed, she should be ashamed of herself, for everyone is scurrying here and there in a most bewildering manner. I have never seen so many fine lords in all my life."

" And there are hundreds more to come before noon," replied Griffith. " My father expects a thousand guests, for all the noblest families throughout Wales have been invited. They are going to stay here for five whole days ! "

" But surely the castle will not hold them all!"
gasped Luned. " It is so full already. I wonder the
castle walls do not bulge out," she laughed.

" Did you not see the men pitching the huge tents
in the park?" replied the boy. " Many of the guests
will sleep there."

" Do tell me what it is all about," begged the little
maid. " Everyone is too busy to stop and talk to me
now."

So in simple fashion Griffith explained how for
many hundreds of years the Welsh and English people
had been at enmity with each other. Now, however,
because a Welshman, Henry Tudor, reigned upon the
throne, peace was established between the two peoples.

" You should know," continued the boy, " it was
my father who helped to place King Henry upon the
throne. For twenty years he has aided him. And so,
in celebration of it all, he is holding this wonderful
festival. Come," he added, " let us return to the
castle."

At the castle gates the two admired a huge strip of
canvas, on which was painted St. George and St.
David embracing each other.

Later in the day, a fine banquet was held in the
great hall.

At the upper end a table, covered in a cloth of crimson velvet, was set apart in the King's honour. Two long tables stretched either side, Sir Rhys occupying the one, while the guests sat at the other.

And now the little girl, Luned, peeping in at one of the doorways, watched a scene that made her hold her breath. The trumpets blared forth, and she saw her companion of the morning carry in gold dishes laden with delicious food. With much dignity, he placed the dishes before the King's empty chair. After a while, he carefully picked up the untouched dishes, and slowly returned them to the kitchens. Finally, the King's vacant chair was turned round, a sign that he had dined, and shortly afterwards, everyone was eating and drinking to his heart's content.

Luned did not stay to listen to the bards sing of the doughty deeds of Sir Rhys, for her nursing woman, sweeping her up in her strong arms, loudly scolded her as she hurried back to their chamber.

Next morning, however, Luned's maid accompanied her upon a steady grey mare to watch the tilting contests. Sir Rhys, resplendent in a suit of golden armour, came riding by amidst his merry-hearted guests, while two hundred retainers, clad in blue livery, followed the company.

Then the sport began. Luned was fascinated as

the players thrust at each other with long lances, and
one after another, the knights tumbled off their horses.

"I am so glad no one is getting hurt," she thought,
for everyone seemed in such high spirits, that when
the tourney was done, winners and losers shook hands
and immediately became the best of friends.

When later, all rode happily home towards the
castle, Griffith invited the maid to ride with him upon
his fine black horse, and he told her how, on the morrow,
he was to play against Sir William Herbert.

"I do hope you'll win," cried Luned. "I'll shout
my loudest for you."

"And forget you are a lady?" laughed the boy.
"Nay," he added, "since my father is the judge, he
will surely award the prize to Sir William, for the loser
is to give a supper at Carmarthen."

The players thrust at each other with their long lances, and one after another, the knights tumbled off their horses.

" And will you invite me?" asked Luned quickly.

" It is too long a journey for a girl," replied he. " Besides, you have seen far too many exciting things already."

So for five days the sporting, hunting and feasting continued, and the country-folk, watching the glorious pageantry that flowed in and out of the castle gates, vowed they had never beheld such gaiety and comradeship amidst so vast a number of people.

Sadly on the fifth day, Luned, from her window, waved a silken handkerchief to Griffith as he rode at the head of the noble company towards Carmarthen.

" Carew Castle will be strangely silent," she murmured.

Already, the tents in the park were lying flat and forlorn on the grass and soon the long bend in the road swallowed up the last galloping horseman.

GEOFFREY EVANS.

RAGLAN

The last years of the reign of Charles I (1625-1649) were years of strife. There were fierce quarrels between King and Parliament which resulted in the first Civil War ; most of Wales was Royalist.

15

WHEN THE KING
LEFT RAGLAN CASTLE

A boy trumpeter stood at the gatehouse of Raglan Castle, his trumpet catching the sun as it blazed with golden light.

He could just glimpse the wide doorway that led from the castle into the courtyard. There was silence everywhere, broken only by short, excited whispers from the groups of men and women whose eyes were fixed upon the doorway.

Bright-eyed servants pushed and jostled each other as they peeped down from every window, for Charles I, Monarch of England, was about to depart from the castle.

" Here come the Duke of Richmond, the Earls of Lindsey and Lichfield—! "

The lines of soldiers stood sharply to attention.

The boy trumpeter sighed. " I wish that the King and his company could stay here for ever ! "

" Pah ! " one of the soldiers muttered. " I would not change my boots for the King's finest buckled shoes ! No, not for all the gold in Wales."

The boy rubbed his trumpet with the edge of his sleeve and looked up inquiringly at the soldier's face.

" Did you not hear the evil news then ? " continued the soldier. " A messenger has just reported that over a thousand Roundhead infantry press this way. They're led by the ' Iron Dwarf.' "

" Col. Morgan ! " gasped the boy.

" Yes, so things will be pretty hot in the castle soon. Hist ! Here comes the King ! " Then he added, " Such haste does not become the King of England ! "

Although the King's face was lined with weariness, he chatted in debonair fashion with his host, the aged Marquis of Worcester. The horses' hooves clopped over the cobbled stones and the boy proudly sounded his trumpet.

" Long life to the King and the Cavaliers ! " came from all sides.

" I wish that all England spoke thus ! " the King smiled, then, reigning in his horse, he turned to the Marquis. " Farewell, my host ! " he cried. " My

As the Marquis came riding bravely by, the boy raised his trumpet to his lips and blew a fine flourish.

visit to Raglan has been a sweet one and yet sad since I feel in my heart it is my last."

So amid loyal cheers, the King set off with his company, and the trumpeter sighed as he watched the gay, sweeping plumes on the broad hats nodding out of sight.

Some time later, it was learned that Roundhead spies were hiding in the cottages nearby, for seventy of the castle horses had mysteriously disappeared. To rout out the spies and to make sure that Roundhead soldiers should not later take cover there, the Marquis had given orders that the villagers must seek shelter within the castle, while his Royalists set fire to every cottage in the neighbourhood.

So early one morning, the villagers, protesting and grumbling, came hurrying into the courtyard of Raglan Castle. Some carried squawking hens, others geese, some drove their pigs before them so that it seemed the bailey had turned into a farmyard. One of the villagers gazed admiringly up at the handsome window of the banqueting hall.

" I think I'll like living here," he confided to his wife.

" Indeed," replied his wife sharply. " I'm not staying here to be blown up by Roundheads ! "

At this moment the boy trumpeter announced the

The reign of Charles I was an era of elegance in dress. Both men and women were richly yet gracefully dressed.

approach of the aged marquis. As his noble, white-haired figure appeared at an upper window, a hush fell upon the noisy rabble in the courtyard.

"First, I ask forgiveness for destroying your homes," he began, and as the muttering and grumbling renewed, he continued, " I now make you two offers. Those of you who wish to stay at the castle until the siege is over are welcome to do so, but money will be given to those who wish to journey from Raglan before the attack begins. Purses have already been made out according to your losses. You may receive them at the Lower Gate."

At such fair offers, the villagers cheered and with one accord hurried to the Lower Gate to receive their due and to make their way to safer quarters.

Afterwards, for several months the Roundheads laid siege to Raglan Castle. They had treacherously dug long tunnels underneath the walls, and by rolling in barrels of gunpowder they intended to blow up the castle. Also, upon the arrival of Sir Thomas Fairfax and his army, such a ruthless attack had been planned that all knew it would be the last.

Before the attack began, Sir Thomas sent peace terms to the castle, and it was promised that if the marquis surrendered, all his Royalist officers and soldiers would be set free. However, there was no mention of pardon for the aged nobleman.

Gathering all his men together, the Marquis cried, " I understand from Sir Thomas Fairfax that this castle of ours is about to be stormed again, and this time it will be such a fearful attack that our walls will not stand. I fear then," he added gravely, " in my duty to you, I must surrender."

" We'll not leave you to the mercy of Fairfax ! " cried an officer.

" There is freedom and life for us,—but what of you ? "

And one and all earnestly begged that they might fight to the last.

But the Marquis gazing fondly upon the many young faces around him shook his head. " I am so old," he said, " I have very little to lose."

So, on a hot August day, the boy trumpeter witnessed another strange scene in the courtyard of Raglan. It was sad to see the castle folk, both of high degree and low, young and old, gathering their possessions together, their eyes so blurred with tears that they left behind what they most cherished, for everyone had grown to love the castle dearly.

Many of the ladies' eyes were red from weeping, but they drew proudly back as Sir Thomas Fairfax and his soldiers rode into the courtyard to take possession.

The marquis, seeing the enemy through the lovely windows of the banqueting hall, slowly arose to meet them. He looked very old and ill, and, perhaps, even then he had learnt that he was to be imprisoned in the grim Tower of London, there to remain until he died.

" Roundheads ride in and Royalists pass out," muttered the trumpeter, sorrowfully. Then, leaping to his feet, he hastened to the spot where he had once stood for the King. As the marquis came riding bravely by, the boy raised his trumpet to his lips and blew a fine flourish.

And a smile lit up the face of the marquis as the trumpet notes rang in his ears. He thought of that dashing, royal figure who had also departed from Raglan for the last time.

PICTON

During the Civil Wars in the 17th century
Picton Castle was at first garrisoned for the
King. (Later it stood for Parliament.)
Legend tells us that in one of the bastions on
the lower storey of the Castle was the nursery
of Sir Richard Phillips' baby son.

16

THE RANSOM OF
A BABY HEIR

In a lower room, in one of the bastions of Picton Castle, a young nurse gently rocked a baby to sleep. Outside the castle walls a cannon boomed, followed by the loud splash of heavy stonework dropping into the moat below. The noise awakened the child and he cried fitfully.

" Hush, hush, my child," soothed the girl and, picking up the baby in her strong arms, she walked to and fro in the small room. " A plague on those Roundheads ! Their guns disturb your slumbers. But they shall not harm you."

She pointed through the window to where Sir Richard Phillips stood with some of his officers. " See," she whispered, " your noble father will not let them touch a hair of your precious head."

As though quietened by the girl's voice, the baby heir lay still again.

In the woods outside the castle the Roundheads piled up their ammunition and pointed their great cannons towards the walls of the Royalist fortress that had so bravely withstood their attack.

" Indeed," cried one soldier, " this delay does not suit my taste. What does it profit us to remain here wasting our powder on such ramparts."

" O for an honest hand-to-hand fight again ! " sighed another. " I'm weary o' this waiting. The days pass and still no news comes of Sir Richard's surrender."

" Surrender ! " exclaimed one. " Why, my lord dares not surrender. Do you not know that his baby son lies within yonder walls ? He'll fight to the end to protect him, for I hear he is uncommon proud of the boy."

" What ! A babe lies within the castle ! By my sword, he has started his soldiering days at a tender age, eh ? "

The Roundhead's face darkened. " Take heed ! " he muttered as he beckoned to the others to draw close around him. " I have a plot that will force my lord to surrender ! Listen ! " And as the soldiers bent their heads together, their leader unfolded his treacherous plan.

Some minutes later, the guns ceased firing and the woods around the castle became hushed again. The

The Roundhead reached up in his stirrups and swiftly snatched the babe from the girl's arm.

nurse, inside the baby's room, timidly opened the window and peered out into the sunlit courtyard. The baby laughed in the warmth of the sun and kicked his sturdy limbs.

" Peace at last ! " breathed the girl. " I wonder what is happening ! Indeed our ears are so accustomed to the noise of battle that this silence is strange."

She could see Sir Richard and his men running towards the stone stairway that led up to the battlements.

" A truce ! A truce ! " cried a Royalist soldier, then as he beheld the girl's white face at the nursery window he called out, " Do not be afraid. The Roundheads seek peace with us ! Ho, ho, we have been more than a match for the traitors ! "

As he, too, hurried after the others to gaze out upon the scene beyond the castle walls, the nurse heard the drawbridge being lowered, and she beheld a Roundhead soldier riding into the empty courtyard. She drew back in alarm, and was about to secure the window, when she perceived that the horseman bore the white flag of peace, while he held a letter aloft in his right hand.

Cautiously, she opened the window wide and watched. The Roundhead wheeled about as though undecided what to do, then, seeing the girl at the lower window, he sped towards her.

Made familiar by Vandyck's paintings — a man dressed in the fashion of 1640 or thereabouts.

The girl's eyes shone with excitement. An honour indeed, to be the first to receive the important news ! Clutching the child in her one arm, proudly and eagerly she bent from the window to take the letter. But as she did so, the Roundhead reached up in his stirrups and swiftly snatched the babe from the girl's arm. Before the terrified girl could raise the alarm, the horseman had flung his cloak over the child and madly careering out from the castle, galloped towards the Roundhead camp.

" Treachery ! "

After one brief spell of bewilderment, cries of alarm and dismay echoed throughout the castle. Fearing to think what harm might befall the child, everyone bewailed the loss of the young heir to the castle, while Sir Richard was beside himself with grief.

" My lord," cried an officer, " it is the wish of every soul here that we surrender this castle to the Roundheads, an act which we pray will induce the traitors to deal mercifully towards the child."

Even as he spoke, there came a message from without, saying, that unless the castle were instantly delivered, the child would be put to death.

Horrified at such a cruel threat, immediate orders were given that all should leave the castle, and so Sir Richard and his company rode out from Picton.

The Roundhead general was so deeply moved when later he heard of the treacherous means by which Sir Richard had been forced to surrender, that instead of allowing his soldiers to destroy the castle, as was their custom, he commanded that Picton should remain untouched and unspoiled amidst the beauty of the surrounding woodlands.

And in the meantime, Sir Richard, having ridden into the enemy's camp, thankfully rescued his little son, who, smiling his approval, seemed well pleased with his first adventure on horseback.

CHEPSTOW

Chepstow took part in the first and second Civil Wars in the 17th century. Sir Nicholas Kemeys, like many other brave Royalists, gave his life for the King's cause.

17

THE GALLANT ROYALIST
OF CHEPSTOW

You can read in Pepys' Diary about the rich glittering fashions of this period.

At the stroke of twelve one April night, in the year 1648, a small party of men stealthily approached the Western Gate of Chepstow Castle.

The night was so still, they could plainly hear the ripple of the river Wye as it flowed far beneath the castle walls. The leader of the men, towering head and shoulders above the others, knocked softly upon the great oaken door.

" Open in the name of the King ! "

Immediately, there came the grating of the portcullis as it was slowly raised and the muffled noise of heavy iron bolts being drawn across. After what seemed an endless time, the door creaked and groaned and was cautiously opened.

"All is well! The garrison is asleep!" murmured a trembling voice.

There were a few hurried whispers and then the men followed their stalwart leader into the dimness of the castle courtyard.

A short while afterwards, the silence was broken by loud cries of amazement and by the shuffling footsteps of struggling soldiers as they were driven down to the castle dungeons.

"Royalists!" cried one. "Led by a giant!"

"You'll pay dearly for this!" shouted another. "You're mad to think you can do this to Cromwell's garrison."

Then came the laughing reply from the tall leader, "Ho, ho, I wish I could see his face when he hears of it."

The fearless leader was a brave Cavalier named Sir Nicholas Kemeys, and his men were staunch Royalists, for these were the days of the Civil Wars when the capturing of a castle meant a stronghold for either Royalist or Roundhead troops.

Next morning, when the Roundhead flag was cast into the Wye and the King's colours waved bravely above the battlements, everyone talked of the daring of Sir Nicholas and his men. Before noon that day, a

Roundhead horseman, galloping with all haste, was well on his way to report the deed to Cromwell.

" I'll return myself to Chepstow ! " cried Cromwell, angrily, when the news reached him. " I'll blow the castle to pieces before Royalists shall thus trick me. We'll bombard them until their battlements come hurtling about their heads ! "

Mustering large forces of men, Cromwell, in high wrath, returned to Chepstow, and in his wake followed heavy wagons laden with shot and cannon. But he did not then know of the dauntless spirit of the men within the castle, nor the strength of those grey battlements.

" By my sword," he muttered as the Roundheads attacked night and day, and still the Royalists showed no signs of weakening, " I'll drain Wales of all her Ironsides before I'll be laughed at in this fashion."

Daily, fresh forces laden with ammunition poured into Chepstow through the narrow gateway of the town, and Sir Nicholas, watching from one of the castle towers, grimly wondered how long he could hold out against them.

But there was a more serious enemy than gunpowder, for, as the weeks passed by, the food supply grew less and less.

Towering above them, Sir Nicholas fought desperately.

" I fear, my lord," cried one of the officers, " if the Roundheads cannot blow us out, they will starve us into surrender."

" Courage," replied Sir Nicholas. " Have you forgotten the boat ? When all seems lost we will escape under cover of darkness across the Wye."

The boat of which he spoke was safely moored to the rocks below the castle walls. At this point, the Wye was so wide and the current so strong that the

131

Royalists thought it a place of safety. But that night, a Roundhead, swimming with powerful strokes, a gleaming knife between his teeth, reached the spot. The blade flashed in the moonlight, the moorings of the boat were cut and the Roundhead swung the boat adrift.

Next morning, news was brought to Sir Nicholas that the boat had vanished, and with it all hope of escape.

" Then we will die fighting for our King," cried Sir Nicholas.

At that moment, there came a deafening crash and Sir Nicholas, running into the courtyard, beheld to his horror, a breach in the walls, low enough for a Roundhead to walk through.

Sir Nicholas stood his ground, expecting any moment to see the enemy rush in upon them. There was a strange hush, for the guns had ceased firing, and into the breach stepped a Roundhead messenger.

" Cromwell commands that this castle be surrendered and that you, my lord, beg for mercy for yourself and your men."

Proudly Sir Nicholas made reply, " If we can march from this castle with the honours that are our due, we will do so. But, upon my life, I will never crave mercy from traitors ! "

At this, the Roundheads came pouring in through the breach upon the valiant men within. Towering above them, Sir Nicholas fought desperately, and the Roundheads marvelled at his strength.

As they closed in upon him, however, Sir Nicholas sank to the ground, his sword raised aloft. " King Charles to the end ! " he cried.

If ever you visit Chepstow Castle you may see the spot where this gallant Cavalier was slain.

Although the stories in this book do not touch the eighteenth century, this illustration is included to show the rich, colourful style of dressing popular during the first George's reign.